Write

Science Fiction

in 5 Simple Steps

Creative Writing
in 5 Simple Steps

Michael A. Schuman

Enslow Publishers, Inc.
40 Industrial Road
Box 398
Berkeley Heights, NJ 07922
USA
http://www.enslow.com

Library of Congress Cataloging-in-Publication Data

Schuman, Michael.
    Write science fiction in 5 simple steps / Michael A. Schuman.
        p. cm. — (Creative writing in 5 simple steps)
    Summary: "Divides the creative writing process into five steps, from inspiration to publishable story, and
includes in-depth treatment of the science fiction genre with writing prompts"—Provided by publisher.
    Includes bibliographical references and index.
    Includes webliography.
    ISBN 978-0-7660-3844-8
    1. Science fiction—Authorship—Juvenile literature. 2. Creative writing—Juvenile literature. I. Title. II.
Title: Write science fiction in five simple steps.
    PN3377.5.S3S28 2012
    808.3'8762—dc22
                            2010045199

Future editions:
Paperback ISBN 978-1-4644-0102-2
ePUB ISBN 978-1-4645-1009-0
PDF ISBN 978-1-4646-1009-7

Printed in the United States of America

032012 Lake Book Manufacturing, Inc., Melrose Park, IL

10 9 8 7 6 5 4 3 2 1

Contents

Book Key

Keeping a Journal

On the Web

Genre History

Fun Fact

Check It Out!

Writer's Block

Here's an Idea!

Your Assignment

Organizer

Daydreaming

Step 1

Inspiration

Boston-based writer M. T. Anderson was at a party in New York City. One guest was an editor named David Gale. Gale was planning to put together a collection of stories to benefit a campaign for literacy. The editor asked Anderson if he was interested in contributing a story to the collection.

On the train back to Boston, Anderson noticed a constant clatter of cell phone conversations. Anderson could not help but overhear some. Just about all were on unimportant topics—subjects that could have waited to be discussed in person. They were about things like one's dating life, another's weekend plans, and someone else's home office decorations.

That inspired Anderson to come up with a plot about a time in the future when people will have direct computer feeds into their brains. He decided it would not be about mere communication between people. He would also make points about advertising, fashion, and entertainment magazines and "all the things the media demand we become."[1]

Anderson decided there was a lot to write about. He had so much in mind that he needed more words than a short story would allow. He knew what he wanted to say would have to be in the form of a book. That's what inspired Anderson to write the science-fiction novel *Feed*.

# What Is Science Fiction?

Many people think of science fiction as stories about spaceships and rockets. And they are correct—to a degree. That is a form of science fiction known as space fiction.

Science fiction can be about all sorts of other topics. These could include robots, clones, computer technology, cyborgs, or life under the ocean, to name a few. The genre of science fiction consists of stories about ideas based on real scientific principles. Science fiction sometimes takes readers to other worlds. On other occasions, it takes readers to an alternative version of Earth.

Some confuse science fiction with fantasy. Sci-fi writer Robert J. Sawyer explains:

> *Remember, science fiction must be believable; it's not the same thing as fantasy. Science fiction is about things that really could happen. (Spaceships really exist and aliens might.) But fantasy is about things that never could happen. There's no such thing as magic or vampires.*
>
> *That said, science fiction is not really about the future—it's about the present. Find something in the real world you're concerned about (such as the environment getting worse or the rights of native peoples) and tell a*

story about that set on another world or in the future to make your point. The movie Avatar *is a good example of this.*[2]

Sometimes the line between science fiction and fantasy is blurred. H. G. Wells's *The Time Machine* has often been referred to as one of the greatest science-fiction stories. However, there is no scientific principle explaining time travel. So *The Time Machine* should really be considered fantasy. But the hero uses a machine, rather than something simple such as a snap of the fingers, to propel him through time. The use of a complex machine is the key that makes critics put *The Time Machine* in the sci-fi category.

Other experts say that science fiction is a form of fantasy. And they put science fiction into two categories: hard science fiction and soft science fiction. Hard science fiction would include *Feed,* based on purely scientific principles. Soft science fiction would include *The Time Machine,* with its concept of time travel.

Finding Your Story

So what do you want to write about? Sci-fi author Bob Howe offers a simple way to get started: "Write what you see; what you hear; what you think; what you feel. Never mind what anybody tells you, or what you see on television or in a movie, or even what you read in a book. Your direct experience is your universe, and no one can write about that but you."[3]

Great Science-Fiction Books

H. G. Wells—*War of the Worlds*
Hostile Martians invade Earth.

Jules Verne—*20,000 Leagues Under the Sea*
A submarine takes a professor through an underwater world in the nineteenth century.

Douglas Adams—*The Hitchhiker's Guide to the Galaxy*
The humorous and dangerous space travels of a man and his companion.

George Orwell—*1984*
In a futuristic world, the Ministry of Truth decides what is right and wrong.

Ray Bradbury—*Fahrenheit 451*
A dark future where no one is allowed to read books.

Michael Crichton—*The Andromeda Strain*
Biological warfare.

E. E. "Doc" Smith—*E. E. "Doc" Smith's Classic Lensman Series*
The first set of science-fiction novels.

Arthur C. Clarke—*2001: A Space Odyssey*
A computer named Hal aboard a spaceship develops a mind of its own.

Aldous Huxley—*Brave New World*
Life in a Utopian state isn't as it should be.

Lois Lowry—*The Giver*
A twelve-year-old boy discovers a dark reality about the world he lives in.

William Gibson—*Neuromancer*
Trouble in a high-tech underworld.

Isaac Asimov—*I, Robot*
Showcases a new world inhabited by robots.

Philip K. Dick—*Do Androids Dream of Electric Sheep?*
Rogue androids and humans meet on Mars.

Great Science-Fiction Films

Planet of the Apes (1968)
Astronauts visit a future world where apes are the masters and humans are the animals.

2001: A Space Odyssey (1968)
An adaptation of Arthur C. Clarke's book.

Star Wars (1977)
The lives of Luke Skywalker, Han Solo, Darth Vader, R2-D2, and the rest. Followed by two sequels and three prequels.

E.T.: The Extra-Terrestrial (1982)
A boy befriends a gentle alien stranded on Earth.

Tron (1982)
A computer expert is trapped inside a giant video game. Followed by one sequel.

Back to the Future (1985)
A comedy/adventure about a teenager transported back in time who accidentally meets his parents when they were teenagers. Followed by two sequels.

The Matrix (1999)
Computers take over the world. Followed by two sequels.

Wall-E (2008)
An animated tale of the future in which the only resident of Earth is a lonely robot.

Avatar (2009)
A Marine assigned to help mine a distant planet is conflicted between his duty and the gentle native people.

Inception (2010)
Corporate spies gather information while in dream states and encounter trouble.

It is one thing to say, "I'm going to write about robots." But how does one take the general idea of robots and turn it into a story? One of the best ways is to read. Take a look at articles in newspapers and magazines, or on trustworthy Web sites. You might read an article about auto factories replacing human workers with robots that do the same jobs without having to be paid. Let your imagination run wild with that idea.

Another way to come up with an idea is to observe, like M. T. Anderson did on his train ride. You could be at a friend's house watching him or her play with their Wii™. What would happen if the Wii seized control of the person, instead of the person controlling the Wii? Or let's say you are in your backyard and you see an airplane fly overhead. Think about what could possibly happen if the airplane flew into another dimension, or another world, inhabited by another race of people. Are they friendly or mean? How would the passengers and crew first react upon being thrust into this strange world? What if these alien creatures are friendly but the crew and passengers don't realize that at first? There are all sorts of possibilities you can take from this basic plot line to make a story.

As an example, let's consider a basic good versus evil story, based on the idea of robot workers in car factories. Let's say a greedy auto factory owner implants special computer chips into the robots in order to make them work harder and faster. Also in the chips are parts that give the robots emotions. That allows them to reason as human beings do.

Seeing what he has done, the factory owner then plants other computer chips into the humans' brains, taking away the part of their brain that gives them the ability to reason. What would happen if the robots suddenly had that power and the human workers turned into robotic clones, taking orders from the robots? The humans suddenly work for no pay and can't afford to take care of their families. Could a flawed chip planted into a renegade human cause that human to realize what has happened? He might become determined to fight back.

The Message

No matter what the subject matter is—robots, aliens, or clones—most science-fiction stories have a theme, or message. And that theme almost always has to do with the nature of people. Nearly all science-fiction stories have people as both main and supporting characters. The stories have some connection to how we humans live, or how we think, or how we act when endangered or threatened with a new kind of progress we don't fully understand.

The theme can be oppression, as in *Avatar*. It can be power run amok, as it is in the novel *The House of the Scorpion* by Nancy Farmer. In Farmer's novel, a young cloned boy named Matt has been created solely to provide spare human parts for a powerful drug dealer. In M. T. Anderson's story *Feed,* the theme is how we humans can let technology take over our lives.

So in addition to fast-paced action, nail-biting drama, or even comic relief, nearly every science-fiction story has a message about people. As you come up with ideas for plot lines, take time to consider what the effects of the story's events would be on people like yourself. That is your theme, or message.

Of course, not all science-fiction stories have messages. Some are written just for fun. There is nothing wrong with that. It all depends on what you want to do with your idea.

Keeping a Journal

Keep a journal of possible story ideas. These should include ideas inspired by articles you read about true science online or in print publications. The journal should also include ideas that pop into your head as you go about your day. After you have seven or eight ideas, look back at them. Decide which has the greatest potential for an original and fascinating story.

Step 2

Research and Preparation

If a fully written story is an oak tree, an idea is just the seed. How do you turn the seed into an oak tree?

If you are writing a story about your experience being bullied by mean kids—or about a youngster playing on a sports team on which every other player is bigger than he is—the answer is easier than writing science fiction. You start by writing about what you know. It is even easier if you are writing a fantasy story. If you want to write a story about a man or woman that can turn into an animal to attack bad guys, you don't have to worry about scientific facts. There are none. The action takes place in a world you have created in your mind.

However, it is important to remember that science fiction is based on the rules of science. A writer can take that one step further. He or she can discuss in a story a scientific principle that is not true yet, but could be in the future. Scientists today have the technology to send a human being to the moon and return him or her to Earth safely. We do not have the technology to send a person to the planet Saturn and return him or her safely home. But it is possible that humans could develop that capability in the future.

Ideas for Ideas

Where do sci-fi writers get their ideas? Some critics say there are only a handful of basic plots. One is man versus nature. A second is the fish out of water, or a person alone in an alien society. A third is opposites attract. That idea obviously works well in romances. But it also works well in action or science-fiction stories in which two people of opposite personalities are paired together on a mission. A fourth is the underdog fighting against all odds. This works especially well in sports movies, but it can also work well in science fiction. Another is the quest, or a person striving to reach an elusive goal.

A sixth plot line is very basic and common in science fiction: good versus evil. The 2009 blockbuster *Avatar* has the same basic good versus evil plot as the 1990 western movie *Dances With Wolves,* but with a twist: the people who resemble us, who we assume to be the good guys don't turn out to be so.

Australian science-fiction writer Sean Williams suggests a basic idea. He says, "My advice to all young or new writers is the same in any genre: read what you love, first of all, and then write what you love. Everything else (finishing, editing, finding a market, etc.) can wait. If you love what you're writing, it will show, and chances are readers will love it too."[1]

So if you are going to write science fiction, you have to know your facts. You cannot have a space traveler landing on Jupiter and drinking water from a stream. Scientists know there is no running water on Jupiter. How does one get the facts? He or she has to do research.

Are there any ways scientists could adapt climates on other planets to support human life? If not, your story should take place in another galaxy where such a planet might exist. We just may not have discovered it yet.

If you want to write about a human colony living under the sea, you will have to discover what, if any, equipment exists now—or may exist in the future—to support life underwater. If you want to write about robots going hay-wire or computers taking on lives of their own, you should know about the basic mechanics of robots or computer construction. Obviously, this is more difficult than writing about a kid your age that runs into bullies at school.

Where to Go

So where does one go to conduct the research he or she needs to write a believable science-fiction story? Start with your school library or public library. The nonfiction sections will have books on diverse scientific subjects. If you can't find any books to your liking, consider looking at past issues of magazines and newspapers that may have published articles on a subject that interests you. Encyclopedias are always a good option for detailed information. Should you not be able to find what you need, do not be shy about asking the library staff. That is what they are there for, and they would be more than happy to help. They have heard requests for information on just about any topic that exists.

Another wonderful source is the Internet. Simply do a search on robots or space travel or whatever grabs you as a possible subject for your story. Please keep in mind, however, that not all Web sites are reliable or even slightly accurate. The majority of books, magazine articles, newspaper articles, and encyclopedias are written by way of a strict process. Fact-checkers and numerous editors read and reread the material to make sure it is accurate. If they have any questions, or if something sounds too unusual to be true, they will ask the author to double-check the statement. Only after books, periodicals, and reference materials are checked as closely as possible, are they published.

On the other hand, anybody can set up a Web site. Some sites are even full of misinformation. The best sites are probably the ones run by colleges and universities. They have very helpful information for young people on all kinds of subjects. You just have to be careful about what you read. The best way to know if a Web site is reliable is to ask a librarian or a teacher.

That leads to a third source for scientific information: teachers at your school. Ask a teacher if you can meet him or her after school to discuss a topic that intrigues you. Many will be flattered and pleased to share their knowledge. If they cannot help you on a certain subject, they will likely recommend a teacher that can. Or they may suggest a good book or Web site.

But research in any science-fiction story extends beyond the scientific principles. Do research on your characters. What is life like in the place your characters live? If your main character works in an auto factory in Michigan, he or she obviously won't be wearing T-shirts and shorts in January. If he or she works in a citrus fruit plant in Florida, then they might.

Explore the typical foods people like to eat in different parts of the country. Your Michigan resident might enjoy munching on a slice of Detroit-style deep-dish square pizza or a Coney Island hot dog. If you provide vivid descriptions of specific local treats, such as the savory chili and biting onions sliding off the hot dog bun, your reader would almost be able to taste it.

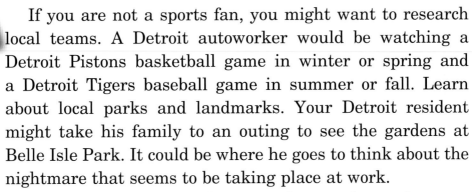

If you are not a sports fan, you might want to research local teams. A Detroit autoworker would be watching a Detroit Pistons basketball game in winter or spring and a Detroit Tigers baseball game in summer or fall. Learn about local parks and landmarks. Your Detroit resident might take his family to an outing to see the gardens at Belle Isle Park. It could be where he goes to think about the nightmare that seems to be taking place at work.

The best places to do this type of research are the same places you would research scientific topics: libraries and the Internet. Nonfiction books about states and cities can be found at your local library. Travel books and Web sites can inform you about local landmarks your character may visit. The more personal touches you have, the more realistic your characters will be to your readers.

Write It Down!

While you are researching, be sure to take notes in your journal. It is likely that while you are researching, you will come up with new ideas for your story. You might even come up with ideas for a different story—either a completely new story you might write in the future, or one you want to write now instead of the story you started out with! Whatever the case, write it down and you won't have to worry about forgetting something important later.

Step 3

Organizing

Now you have a basic story idea. But how do you turn that into a fully detailed, engrossing story? If you write your story now, it might be no more than two or three paragraphs. The next step is to establish the setting, create conflict, and flesh out your characters.

Setting

First of all, think about your setting. As a writer of science fiction, you have a lot of freedom to create a wild and fantastic world. People that write nonfiction and realistic fiction do not have that luxury. Think about what would be the best time and place to make your theme most profound and your action most vivid. Is your world planet Earth or a distant planet in another galaxy? Is it under the ocean or inside the human body? When does your story take place—today, 20,000 years in the future, or 20,000 years in the past? If you're feeling especially ambitious, you can even have your story take place in various galaxies or during many different points in history, if it involves space or time travel.

In many ways, when a person writes an original story, he or she is creating a whole new world (or universe!). If this sounds intimidating, don't worry. All you need to do is ask yourself some basic questions and follow your imagination, but always remember to keep it believable in the context of your story.

You may already know when you first start writing that the story will take place in an auto factory in Michigan or a citrus plant in Florida. These are fairly specific places. Before you start detailing these places, ask yourself about the whole planet Earth. Is Earth in your story the same Earth on which we live? If not, then how is it different? Is the political environment the same? Who is president of the United States? Have any other countries in your story changed at all? The answers to these questions would obviously have some effect on Michigan, Florida, or any other more specific places you're writing about.

Not all the answers to the questions you ask will prove important to your story. Some may wind up having no bearing on your story at all. Still, just by asking and answering them for yourself, they can make the story stronger. The more you know about your setting and background as the writer, the more real it will likely feel to your reader. It is also much easier to flesh out these details before you start than it would be if you needed to fill them in later. (And if you do find inspiration to put new things in your story from such questions, then all the better!)

Conflict

After you establish your setting, think of events and conversations that should happen to make your story take shape. Always keep in mind that every good story needs conflict. Conflict is what makes your readers want to read your story through to the conclusion. That is true whether the main character's adversaries are aliens, robots, or fellow human beings. The main character's conflicts can be small at first. Then they should build to a climax just before the ending.

Sci-fi writer John D. Brown offers this tip:

> *It doesn't matter where you start when you invent a story, but you need to end up with a character you think is fun, cool, or interesting, that has a problem other people will find funny or compelling—that's the core of your story. The problem can be a mystery the character needs to solve (there are strange green lights in the sewer), a danger or threat to some aspect of the character's happiness or someone they care about (holy smokes, that big alien that looks like a bug wants to eat my head), or an opportunity for something that will make them happy.*[1]

Remember that every action taken by your main character has to have a consequence, either good or bad, that will advance the plot. If he or she lies to a coworker or a best friend, then that must have an effect on what happens later in the story. But as you create a detailed story line, you should also be thinking at the same time about how many characters you need to tell your story.

Organization

Write a basic outline for your story. Perhaps the best way to start an outline is to think about how you want your story to start and how you want it to end. Write those ideas down. Then fill in the middle. After you write down the beginning action, think of other actions that introduce the characters and conflict. About halfway through the story you will want the action to start building toward a climax. The climax should be resolved about four-fifths of the way through the story. The ending should be a way for the main character, and your readers, to catch their breath.

Keeping Track of Characters

You will certainly need a main character and his or her nemesis, or rival. You can limit your story to just two characters if that is the best way to make your point. Most science-fiction stories have more than two main characters, though. The hero and the villain will likely have friends. These friends might support the hero or villain throughout the story, or they might turn on them. Either way, their actions—like all other actions—must advance the plot. If as you develop your story you find that a character's actions are not advancing the plot, it might be best to get rid of that character.

As you develop your characters, be sure to give them distinctive traits. Are they shy? Are they religious? What are their hobbies? Do they get angry easily or do they tend to be patient? Would they rather watch sports or play a sport? Would they rather hang out with friends or stay home and read a book? These traits will help turn your characters from one-dimensional stick figures to fleshed-out human beings—or aliens or robots, as the case may be.

Most writers immediately have a good idea of those character traits they feel are important in serving their larger story. But it is a helpful exercise to consider some of the more mundane facts in a character's background, too. Begin by giving each of the characters a specific birth date. Then decide what part of the country (or world or galaxy) they were born. If you have two characters in a story that are good friends, for example, perhaps they are the same age and grew up together in the same place. Or perhaps they're not the same age or from the same place but became friends later, as adults. In either case, even if these facts never come up in your story, it helps to keep them in mind while you're writing. It will likely deepen your characters' relationships and will help what you write feel more natural and real.

This is just as useful if you have two characters who are enemies. Perhaps there is something in their backgrounds that would contribute to the conflict between them. (It is important to note that not all of your characters' conflicts need to build to a battle or a fistfight. Emotional and psychological conflicts are often more dramatic than physical ones.)

You should also create a basic family history for all of your key characters. Do they have brothers or sisters? What are their parents like? You may not see any of this character's family members in the story. They may not even be mentioned. But such facts would still play an important part in each character's history and how each developed his or her personality. This could be useful information to keep in mind during your writing process.

Family histories could also lead to interesting new plot directions. Maybe you have a character that was raised by just one parent, or other relatives entirely. The fate of the missing parent (or parents) could be a mystery. This could then become a plot point in your story. For example, in the original *Star Wars* film, Luke Skywalker is raised by his aunt and uncle and knows very little about his parents. This plays into the character's loneliness and his search for identity beyond his aunt and uncle's farm. It also becomes important in the film series later on, when his true parentage is finally revealed.

Now ask yourself: how will your characters' personalities help advance the plot? Let's go back to our autoworker who is having trouble with robots at his job. He has been trying to convince his bookworm friend who works next to him in the factory that their boss is up to no good. Later on, while your main character is playing softball with a group of friends after work, the coworker is at the library and stumbles upon an old news article detailing how their boss was arrested several years ago for embezzling money from the company.

A common mistake young writers make is to create a hero that is perfect. Nobody—not even Superman—is perfect. (Remember that he is powerless against Kryptonite.) Give your main character flaws. That will make him or her seem more real.

When approaching the story's conclusion, make sure your main character has changed in some way. It is not enough that a problem has been solved, and the bad guy was captured or killed. The main character has to have matured, or otherwise become a better person. For the story to be believable, the main character cannot be the exact same person he or she was at the story's beginning.

Make Writing a Routine

Set up a writing schedule. The best way to accomplish this is to think about 1) what times of day outside of school you feel most productive, and 2) what times of day you are free to write. Obviously, if you have a job, the job is your first priority. Homework is another top priority. You can plan as little as fifteen or thirty minutes to write. But try to meet at least that goal every day. It is tempting to skip weekends, since Saturday and Sunday are regarded as leisure time. However, those may be the best times to set for your writing schedule, since you have fewer school or work distractions.

Writing Vivid Descriptions

Vivid descriptive details are essential to bringing the people, places, and action in your story to life for your readers. Try to describe a place or object to your family or friends without actually saying what it is. Then have them try to guess what you are describing. Begin with simple subjects, such as a pencil or Paris, France. Then go on to more difficult subjects, such as a rare animal or some place very specific, your English classroom, for example.

Step 4

Writing

It seems like this could be a very short chapter. You want to write a story. So start writing. Indeed, when the ideas are flowing in your head like water from a spigot, writing is a very easy task. It's really less like a task than a fun hobby. The ideas come to you and you write them down.

But it is not so easy. Anyone can write a 5,000-word story. But not anyone can write a good 5,000-word story. And even fewer can write an excellent 5,000-word story.

Once you begin writing, you may face several problems. There are going to be days when the words don't flow endlessly out of your computer keyboard. You may be at a loss for ideas. But I have an outline, you may think. However, you may be at a point where your outline is not working. Your story may not be heading in the same direction as the original outline does. You may have discovered that it makes more sense for your characters to take actions that are not in the outline. Perhaps the story should be heading in a totally different direction.

It could be that one of the supporting characters you developed does not seem to have a real purpose. His or her actions are not pushing the story forward. Yet you have already introduced that character, and he or she has already interacted several times with the main character. So what do you do? Cutting that character means rewriting much of the story. It is like taking apart a half completed jigsaw puzzle and starting all over again. It is painful, but sometimes it must be done in order to help your story.

How does a beginning writer come up with the best words to describe action or relay a character's thoughts? First, always have a thesaurus handy for those times when no matter how hard you think your mind keeps drawing blanks. Computer software comes with thesauruses, and you could also find them on the Internet. Or you can keep an old-fashioned, hard-copy thesaurus near you.

Point of View

Before you start writing, you should decide on your story's point of view. Do you want to tell your story in first, second, or third person? First person is told from the author's point of view: "I am standing in a dingy factory room watching a robot inch toward me." Second person is told from the reader's point of view: "You are standing in a dingy room as a robot inches toward you." Third person is told from the point of view of an omniscient observer—a narrator who sees and tells everything: "Fred is standing in a dingy room as a robot inches toward him."

There is no right or wrong point of view to tell a story. Simply choose what works best for you. The main advantage of first person is that it makes the story more personal. The

Character Traits Chart

Keep a chart of your characters and their traits. If Fred is curious and hardworking, write that down. If Howie is lazy, speaks in phrases as opposed to sentences, and likes watching basketball, write that down. If Sabrina is talkative and full of herself, write that down, too. If the robot Deep 6 is menacing and bold, make sure you note that. You don't want the people, robots, or aliens you created to do things out of character. Your readers would find it unbelievable if for no reason lazy Howie suddenly starts to run sprints after work or school, or if stuck-up Sabrina decides to be too nice by giving another person extra credit for something she did.

reader feels as if he or she is in the main character's head, taking in all the thoughts, emotions, and sensory experiences the main character is living through. The main disadvantage is that the main character can't see everything. If the main character is in a factory, he obviously does not know that ten miles away his boss is living in a mansion, lighting a cigar with a twenty-dollar bill. He is also limited to reporting only those conversations he takes part in or overhears.

The main advantage of third-person narration is that you see everything. In one paragraph, you can describe what your main character is doing. In the next paragraph, you can discuss what is happening in another part of town.

But telling a story from a third-person point of view is less personal than from a first-person point of view. "Fred felt a strange pang of jealousy as he watched the robot do his job," is less personal than, "I felt a strange pang of jealousy as I watched the robot do my job." Putting yourself in the character's shoes creates a more visceral scene.

Telling a story from a second-person point of view is very difficult. Second person works best in a nonfiction, how-to book, such as the one you are reading.

Now that you have chosen the point of view, how do you start your story? It is important that the first chapter should begin with a "hook," or some action that makes the reader want to continue reading. The story can start with a conversation between characters or a vivid description of a setting. It can also start in the middle of some action. Many times, it can be a combination of any of the above.

Nancy Farmer begins *The House of the Scorpion* this way: "In the beginning, there were thirty-six of them, thirty-six droplets of life so tiny that Eduardo could see them only under a microscope. He studied them anxiously in the darkened room."[1] She uses the third-person point of view to invite her readers into a setting. The reader wants to know what these droplets of life are all about.

On the other hand, Will Hobbs begins his novel *Go Big or Go Home* with a setting and a dramatic lead sentence: "There might be more unlikely ways to die, but I can't think of any. It was late in the evening at the end of the first week of August. I was home alone and sitting on the edge of my bed, only seconds from crashing. I let out a huge yawn."[2]

Unlike Farmer, Hobbs tells his story in the first person, through the eyes and feelings of a boy named Brady Steele. As one reads these opening sentences, it is natural to wonder what way of dying is being discussed here. And if the boy is thinking about dying and on the verge of crashing, why does he yawn? Doesn't it make you want to read and find out what's going on?

Show Versus Tell

From here you can start telling your story. Or to be more accurate, you can start showing your story. Don't say simply, "Fred was nervous all day." You can tell the reader about Fred's state of mind more creatively by saying, "Fred had almost twisted his fingers into a knot and had chewed his pencil down to a stub." Showing, rather than telling, gives the reader a more active role in reading your story. In his or her mind, the reader figures out what the description says about Fred. In addition, the reader relates his or her own experiences about being nervous to those of Fred.

The flip side to showing rather than telling is the possibility of adding too much detail, or overwriting. Writers should not use ten-dollar words when ten-cent words will do. Consider this sentence: "The most evil robot, Deep 6, had a dastardly plan that would entail a vile and diabolical scheme, bent on ruining the magnanimous nature of the lowly but benevolent workers."

Getting Unblocked

Every writer gets what is known as writer's block. Some writers experience it more often than others. But don't believe for a minute that even professional writers don't get writer's block. You may be tired. It may be a beautiful day and you would rather be hanging out with your friends than filling a blank computer monitor with words. Or you might want to write, but you simply cannot get into your story on a particular day. The words are not coming to you. You force yourself, but the words you are writing are uncreative or clichéd. The dialogue you are putting into your main character's mouth seems boring. Perhaps the story is starting to appear less interesting to you than when you first envisioned it.

So what do you do? Let's go back to the third sentence of this chapter, the three small words: "So start writing."

Force yourself. Put at least something, no matter how poor it seems at the time, down on paper or on your computer screen. If writing was easy, anyone could do it. But if you already have a story in mind that you want to write, then you are obviously a creative person. Once you have a basic scene written, it is always easier to change it later when you feel more refreshed. You can substitute action that drags with words that carry punch. You can replace boring dialogue with snappier words for your characters to say.

That does not exactly slide off the tongue. How do you think the same message could be stated in a more basic but expressive nature?

You can look at these contrasting writing styles through a metaphor. A woman wearing one set of beautiful beads around her neck can look classy. A woman wearing multiple beads, necklaces, and chokers looks gaudy. You don't want your writing to be gaudy.

Just as I used a metaphor to illustrate my point, you can use metaphors and similes to liven up your writing. In a simile, the writer makes a comparison usually connected by the word "like" or "as." Again, a common error is to overwrite. "The moon was as blue as Delft glass" is simple and to the point.

On the other hand, a metaphor is like a simile but without the word "like" or "as." An example would be, "The moon was a blue balloon that night when Fred went out for a walk."

In *Go Big or Go Home,* Will Hobbs's character Brady Steele, telling his story in first person, describes exploring a cave with this simile: "We followed the passage as it wound back and forth like a sidewinder, up and down like a roller coaster."[3]

Writers must always be careful as well when composing dialogue. Try to make your characters talk the way real people do, but use some creativity. You don't want dialogue to be too heavy-handed. Here are a few examples. "Fred said, 'The factory that night was as cold as the ice cubes that were stuck to the bottom shelf of my freezer since last

New Year's Eve.'" That might be an expressive way for an omniscient narrator to describe a Michigan winter night. However, it is awkward coming out of the mouth of one of your characters. Real people don't usually make such elaborate comparisons unless they're purposely trying to confuse or amuse someone else.

Use some creativity but don't overdo it. "Fred said, 'The factory was freezing that night,'" might be more realistic, but it is too basic to keep your reader's interest. Consider, "Fred said, 'I went inside the factory and it was as cold as last New Year's Eve.'" A simple simile paints a colorful picture for your audience.

In one scene in *The House of the Scorpion,* Nancy Farmer shows that Matt has feelings of self-pity with the following dialogue and action:

> *"You're like a wild animal," complained Maria as she stood in the doorway of Matt's room. "You hide in here like a bear in a cave."*
>
> *Matt looked indifferently at the curtained windows. He liked the safe, comfortable darkness. "I am an animal," he replied. Once these words would have pained him, but he accepted his status now.*
>
> *"I think you just like to wallow," said Maria, striding in to open the curtains and windows.[4]*

Maria's comparing Matt to a wild animal in hiding, specifically a bear holing itself up in its cave, sounds like something you would say to a friend retreating from the world. You understand Matt is going through something, and Maria wants him to snap out of it.

Dialogue

Crafting good, believable dialogue is a skill that writers perfect with practice. However, writing dialogue for a science-fiction story comes with special quirks. If your main character travels to another galaxy and discovers life-forms, he or she will have to communicate with them . . . but how? It is unrealistic that the extraterrestrials will speak modern-day English.

They could speak their own language. But how would your readers understand what they are saying? You could include a glossary to translate their language into English. That would be cumbersome, however. It would make your readers continually stop reading to check the glossary, which would interrupt the flow of the story.

The simplest thing to do is provide a method for your English-speaking characters to translate the extra-terrestrials' language into English. That could be done with something as simple as an old-fashioned hard-copy book, like a French-English dictionary, or something as complicated as a computer-based code that translates the languages.

The other option would be to do nothing regarding translation. Sure, it is unrealistic for extraterrestrials to speak English. Yet they have done so in several science-fiction stories. In the *Star Wars* saga, Luke Skywalker and the gang have always spoken English and few people seem to be bothered by it. If your stories are as good as those in the *Star Wars* saga, perhaps your readers won't be bothered by that either.

Finally, if you are writing a novel, how long should your chapters be and how should they be divided? The best answer is that there is no one answer. Sci-fi writer Orson Scott Card wrote:

> Some writers divide chapters into sections from one character's point of view, so that the chapters change as often as the point of view shifts.
>
> Some writers divide chapters after climactic scenes; others try to end them on cliffhangers or stunning revelations, so that the reader must turn the page and keep going.[5]

It all depends on what works for you.

Stop and Listen

Any time you feel the need for inspiration on writing dialogue, simply step away from your computer and take a walk into the real world. Go to the mall, a school sporting event, or just listen to what classmates are saying in the halls between classes or just before or just after class. Zero in on their patterns and rhythms of speech. Could you make your characters talk in the same manner?

Step 5

Publishing

Your first draft is done. I say "first draft" because no manuscript is ready to be sent to a publisher right after it is first written. That goes for professionals as well as beginners. The manuscript will certainly need editing. There will surely be grammatical errors or awkward phrasing. Dialogue may need to be punched up here or there. Remember those days when you wrote but were not in the spirit. Some of that prose can be made more vivid. Perhaps even some of the plot can use tweaking.

Put the manuscript away for a week. Perhaps even two weeks. Then read it over with fresh eyes. You will be surprised to discover how much of your story can be improved. That is not a reflection of your writing skills. It happens to every writer.

After all, writing is not mathematics. There are no absolute right or wrong answers. Sci-fi author Marshall Payne notes:

> *As to the writing itself, becoming a master craftsman should be every writer's goal. And learning to edit one's own fiction is the perfect place to begin. Developing the ability to parse your sentences and rework them until*

they say exactly what you want them to say should be a joy and not a chore. Learning to write beautiful rock-firm sentences is what separates the pro from the wannabe. Most of us have stories we want to tell, it's developing the craft to tell them that makes the difference.[1]

Another sci-fi writer, David Gerrold, said, "The more you write, the more you learn. You might write a hundred bad stories, but you'll learn something from every one of those bad stories. You'll learn to recognize your own bad habits."[2]

On the other hand, do not wait to submit your story until you feel everything in it is absolutely 100 percent perfect. That won't happen. At some point you have to submit it. No matter how many changes you have made and how much rewriting you have done, chances are likely that after you submit it you will still find something you could have changed. If an editor thinks your story has potential, he or she may very well take a chance with it.

So Where Do You Submit It?

Thanks to the Internet, you have several options that did not exist years ago. One of the best known and most respected sites that take youth sci-fi is Lulu, which allows you to publish your book in a number of options and sizes. It even allows you to select the type of paper you want for your book, as well as the cover.

Teen Ink is both a Web site and a newspaper-style periodical. It has a section on science fiction/fantasy. *Teen Ink* is a project of the Young Authors Foundation, an organization founded in 1989. On the *Teen Ink* Web site, the foundation states its philosophy: "The Young Authors Foundation feels strongly that one of the greatest needs of young people is to preserve their sense of self-worth. *Teen Ink*'s role is to listen to its contributors and provide a forum in which teens can express themselves through poetry, essays, stories, reviews, art and photography."

A third option is Page to Fame, operated by a Web site titled WEbook. Writers submit their work and readers rate it. There is a submission fee for writers. Yet another possibility is Ink Pop. Ink Pop states that their "ultimate goal is to find the next big thing in teen lit, and the ultimate prize in every aspiring author's dream: a publishing contract."

It is important to do your best, but not to raise your hopes too high. Even the best-selling and most critically acclaimed writers had to deal with rejections at first. In addition, be careful of scams. Just as there are people that compose Web sites filled with false information, there are always those who want to take advantage of young writers. When looking into submitting a work to any Web site, you might want to Google its name, or perhaps you might Google the name of one of its writers. Then read what others have had to say about their experiences.

You might also want to read, with the help of a parent or a teacher, warnings about scams that take advantage of writers of all ages. The Web site of the Science Fiction and Fantasy Writers of America, a group of professional writers, features a section on scams.

Of course, you can try to get published the old-fashioned way—through a publisher that still prints hard copy books. Even in this age of the Internet, there are many traditional publishing companies looking for talented writers. The best source is *The Writer's Market,* published and updated yearly by Writer's Digest Books based in Cincinnati, Ohio.

Regardless, don't be scared to take a chance. As one sci-fi writer certainly must have exclaimed many years ago, "The sky's the limit!"

Having Your Work Critiqued

Some writers ask others to read their manuscripts and comment on them. If you do, be sure you give it to someone whose opinion you trust. It could be a friend or a parent. But do not give it to a person who will say everything is great just to spare your feelings. Have you ever watched the tryout episodes of *American Idol*? Think how many people are panned by the judges because they can't sing a single note. These failed entrants often respond the same way: "My parents and/or my best friends say I am a great singer."

However, you don't want to give your manuscript to a person who tends to be overly critical or someone that does not understand science fiction either. A friend or relative that understands science fiction would be best. So would an English teacher—but again, only if the teacher appreciates science fiction. A teacher that is an expert in nineteenth-century English literature would not be a good choice—even if he or she is a great English teacher.

It is your choice to do what you want with the criticism you are given. Try not to take negative remarks personally. Keep an open mind. Sometimes the person may be right on the money with a comment about a plot twist that does not move the story forward or a character that does not seem to be needed. But in the end, it is your choice. You can use your gut feeling to overrule any criticism.

Chapter Notes

Step 1: Inspiration

1. Kathleen Horning, "Yes Indeed, the British Are Coming," *School Library Journal,* November 1, 2006, <http://www.schoollibraryjournal.com> (April 25, 2010).

2. Personal e-mail from Robert J. Sawyer, September 27, 2011.

3. Personal e-mail from Bob Howe, September 27, 2011.

Step 2: Research and Preparation

1. Personal e-mail from Sean Williams, September 27, 2011.

Step 3: Organizing

1. Personal e-mail from John D. Brown, September 27, 2011.

Step 4: Writing

1. Nancy Farmer, *The House of the Scorpion* (New York: Simon Pulse, 2004), p. 2.

2. Will Hobbs, *Go Big or Go Home* (New York: HarperCollins Publishers, 2008), p. 1.

3. Ibid., p. 130.

4. Farmer, p. 92.

5. Orson Scott Card, "Uncle Orson's Writing Class: Chapter Length," *Hatrack River,* April 1, 2004, <http://hatrack.com/writingclass/lessons/2004-04-01-1.shtml> (September 22, 2011).

Step 5: Publishing

1. Personal e-mail from Marshall Payne, September 28, 2011.

2. John Hanley, Jr., "Interview With David Gerrold," *Finding My Way,* n.d., <http://www.findingmywaymovie.com/davidgerrold.html> (September 21, 2011).

Glossary

android—A robot that is designed and built to resemble a human being.

climax—The point of greatest conflict in a short story or novel, just before the turning point occurs.

clone—An exact duplicate of a human being, grown from a cell of that human being.

conflict—Opposing aims between main characters in a short story or novel.

cyborg—A human being that has a part (or parts) of his or her body replaced with mechanical or electrical parts.

fantasy—A genre of literature in which magical, otherworldy occurrences take place. These occurrences are usually unexplainable by science.

galaxy—A collection of planets, stars, and other material in space that all orbit a common center of mass.

hard science fiction—Science fiction based purely on scientific principles.

metaphor—A comparison of one object to another without using the words *like* or *as*.

nonfiction—Writing based on true events.

plot—The basic story line in a novel or short story.

realistic fiction—A work of literature based on events that could actually occur in the world as we know it.

simile—A comparison of one object to another using the words *like* or *as*.

soft science fiction—A work of science fiction that combines both scientific and fantasy elements.

theme—The underlying message of a work of literature.

thesaurus—A reference book or Web site listing synonyms and antonyms.

Further Reading

Books

Athans, Philip, and R. A. Salvatore. *The Guide to Writing Fantasy and Science Fiction: 6 Steps to Writing and Publishing Your Bestseller!* Avon, Mass.: Adams Media, 2010.

Farrell, Tish. *Be a Creative Writer*. Tunbridge Wells, Kent, England: TickTock Books, Ltd., 2010.

Hamilton, John. *You Write It: Science Fiction*. Edina, Minn.: ABDO and Daughters, 2009.

Smith, Pamela Jaye. *The Power of the Dark Side: Creating Great Villains, Dangerous Situations, and Dramatic Conflict*. Studio City, Calif.: Michael Wiese Productions, 2008.

Internet Addresses

County of Los Angeles Public Library Science Fiction For Kids
http://www.colapublib.org/reading/children/sci-fi.html

Cynthia Leitich, Children's and YA Science Fiction Novels
http://www.cynthialeitichsmith.com/lit_resources/favorites/by_genre/science_fic.html

Science Fiction and Fantasy Writers of America
http://www.sfwa.org/

Addendum

Useful Web Sites

Here are some of the top Web sites for accurate scientific information:

National Aeronautics and Space Administration
http://www.nasa.gov/

National Geographic Society
http://www.nationalgeographic.com/

National Institutes of Health
http://www.nih.gov/

National Oceanic and Atmospheric Administration
http://www.noaa.gov/

Smithsonian Institution
http://www.si.edu/

European Space Agency
http://www.esa.int/esaCP/index.html

Writing Contests

There are many writing contests for young people. Here is a selection:

WARNING: The Science Fiction and Fantasy Writers of America warns all writers to be cautious about supposed contests that are little more than scams. Please go to this link for more details: http://www.sfwa.org/for-authors/writer-beware/contests/

The James White Award, no age restrictions
http://www.jameswhiteaward.com/

The Scott Imes Award, open to all ages
http://www.geekpartnership.org/evt_writingContest.htm

WillyCon Short Story/Poetry Contest, for all ages
http://wildcat.wsc.edu/clubs/willycon/gen/short_story/

Index